Electromagnetism, and How It Works

SCIENTIFIC
AMERICAN

Electromagnetism,
and
How It Works

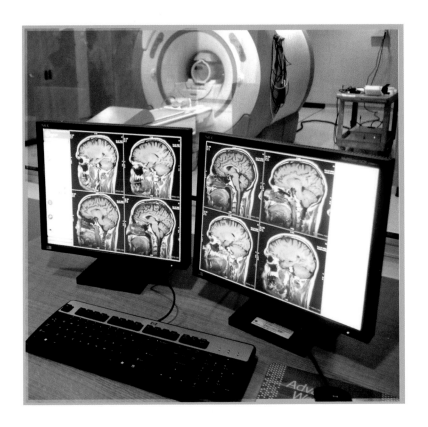

By Stephen M. Tomecek

CHELSEA HOUSE
PUBLISHERS
An imprint of Infobase Publishing

Scientific American: Electromagnetism, and How It Works

Chelsea House
An imprint of Infobase Publishing
132 West 31st Street
New York NY 10001

Library of Congress Cataloging-in-Publication Data

Tomecek, Stephen.
  Electromagnetism, and how it works / Stephen M. Tomecek.
    p. cm. — (Scientific American)
  Includes bibliographical references and index.
  ISBN-13: 978-0-7910-9052-7 (hardcover)
  ISBN-10: 0-7910-9052-3 (hardcover)
  1. Electromagnetism—Juvenile literature. I. Title. II. Series.

  QC760.2.T66 2007
  537—dc22
                                             2007017744

Chelsea House books are available at special discounts when purchased
in bulk quantities for businesses, associations, institutions, or sales
promotions. Please call our Special Sales Department in New York at
(212) 967-8800 or (800) 322-8755.

You can find Chelsea House books on the World Wide Web at
http://www.chelseahouse.com

Series design by Gilda Hannah
Cover design by Takeshi Takahashi and Joo Young An
Illustrations by Melissa Ericksen

Printed in the United States of America

Bang GH 10 9 8 7 6 5 4 3 2 1

This book is printed on acid-free paper.

Contents

CHAPTER ONE

The Magic of Magnets

Take a look around. Can you see any magnets? Unless you're standing in the kitchen and the refrigerator is covered with notes and artwork, the answer is probably no. Yet, even if magnets aren't in sight, they are everywhere. The refrigerator is one example. Most refrigerator doors have a magnetic strip that holds the door closed. Also, the device that keeps the refrigerator's contents cold is powered by an electric motor, which is powered by magnets.

Magnets aren't just found in the kitchen either. Magnets drive the speakers on a stereo. Tape recorders, VCRs, and the hard drives on computers all use magnets, too. In fact, if it weren't for magnets, our world would be a very different place, because almost all of the electricity that is produced by power plants comes from generators, which are loaded with magnets.

The Nature of Magnets

Magnets have a special property, or characteristic, that sets them apart from all other substances in the universe. Magnets are attracted to certain types of metal, such as iron, steel (which is actually made from iron), and cobalt. Magnets also stick to alloys, which are mixtures of various metals. All magnetic alloys have at least one magnetic metal in them. By making an alloy, engineers can create a metal with special properties—for example, a metal that is magnetic but does not rust like iron or steel.

William Gilbert and the Law of Poles

Even though people knew about lodestones for thousands of years, they really didn't understand how magnets worked. This changed with the discoveries of an English scientist named William Gilbert.

NATURE'S OWN MAGNETS

Thousands of years ago—long before people began using magnets for practical purposes—magnetic substances could be found lying on the ground. They didn't look like the ones we use today, though. They were heavy black rocks known as lodestones, which are formed from an iron-rich mineral called magnetite. No one knows who was the first person to discover lodestone. It *is* known that one of the first people to record the mineral's unusual behavior was the Greek philosopher Thales. He was born in about 640 B.C. in a town called Miletus, in modern-day Turkey. According to legend, one of his lodestone samples came from a town called Magnesia. In writing about the rock, Thales called it *ho magnetes lithos*, meaning "the rock from Magnesia." Eventually these unusual rocks became known as magnets.

Lodestone is a naturally occurring type of iron ore. Its magnetic properties have been known for thousands of years. One of its earliest uses was as the basis for primitive Chinese compasses around the fourth century B.C.

In the late sixteenth century, English physician William Gilbert pioneered the science of electricity and magnetism. In his work, *De Magnete*, published in 1600, Gilbert compared the polarity of the magnet to the polarity of the Earth, and noted the similarities and differences between electricity and magnetism.

Gilbert was born in 1544. As a boy, he was interested in nature and the world around him. This came in handy in his future career. Thanks to his family's great wealth, he was able to attend the finest schools—including both Oxford and Cambridge universities, where he studied medicine.

While Gilbert was practicing as a physician, he conducted scientific experiments in his spare time. Many of his early experiments involved alchemy—the old science of trying to transform a common metal into a precious metal. Alchemists worked with different metals, such as iron and lead, in the hope of changing them into gold. It was during these experiments that Gilbert began studying magnets.

Before Gilbert's time, most people thought that magnets attracted metal because they had magical power. They also believed that magnets could be used to cure some health problems, such as headaches. (Today, some people still believe this is true.)

By doing careful tests with lodestones, Gilbert discovered that a magnet's force came in two different forms. Most of the time, if two lodestones were near each other, they would move together. If one stone were turned around, however, the two stones would then push apart, or **repel**. After conducting hundreds of tests on lodestones, Gilbert came to the conclusion that every magnet has two ends that act differently. He would suspend a piece of lodestone by a string, and after swaying for a little while it would always come to rest pointing in the same direction. One end of the stone would point north and the other end would point south. Because the lodestones pointed to the poles of Earth, he called the two ends of a magnet **poles**. Based on this discovery, Gilbert also correctly concluded that Earth itself acts as a giant magnet.

As he continued his tests, he found that if the south poles of two magnets were brought near each other, the magnets would push apart. If he did the same thing with the north poles, they too would push apart. The only time that magnets attracted each other was when the opposite poles of two magnets were brought together. Today this is called the **law of poles**.

Getting Inside a Magnet

Gilbert died in 1603, but not before publishing his discoveries in a fantastic book called *Concerning Magnetism, Magnetic Bodies and the Great Magnetic Earth*. One of the most important pieces of information contained in the book was how to make a magnet.

The metals that a magnet attracts can also be turned into magnets themselves. Gilbert discovered that a piece of iron rubbed along a lodestone would eventually become magnetized, too.

How can a regular magnet turn a plain paper clip into a magnetic paper clip? And how can a lodestone turn an ordinary piece of iron into a magnet? The answer lies in the way the metal in the paper clip and the piece of iron are put together.

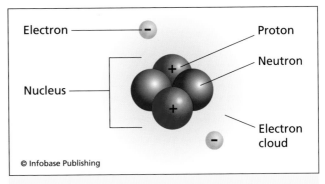

© Infobase Publishing

The center of an atom is called the nucleus. Inside the nucleus are positively charged protons and neutrons that have no charge. Circling around the outside of the nucleus is a cloud of negatively charged electrons.

Everything on Earth is made of tiny particles called **atoms**. Individual atoms cannot be seen, but scientists have learned a lot about them using special pieces of equipment. Scientists have discovered that all atoms are made of two main parts. The central core of the atom is called the **nucleus.** Within the nucleus are two types of particles, called *protons* and *neutrons*. Neutrons have no electric charge, and protons have a positive electric charge.

Moving around the nucleus at very high speed is the second main part of an atom: a cloud of particles called **electrons.** Electrons have a negative electric charge, which means that they are the electrical opposite of protons. As the electrons move around the nucleus, they also spin themselves—similar to the way Earth moves around the Sun. As Earth moves in its orbit, it also rotates like a top.

This electron spin is what helps turn a regular paper clip into a magnet. When an electron spins, it makes a tiny **magnetic field**. You can think of a magnetic field as the area around a magnet where it will attract a magnetic object.

A magnetic field is invisible, but there is a simple way to see one at work. Take a bar magnet and place it on a flat surface. Spread a piece of clear plastic wrap over the magnet, and then sprinkle some iron filings on top of the wrap. The tiny pieces of iron will line up, making a map of the magnetic field. Weak magnets will tend to produce a small magnetic field that shows only a few lines of iron filings. A strong magnet will have a large magnetic field with many lines reaching far from the magnet.

Every magnet has two poles. The direction of these poles and the magnetic field around them is controlled by the direction in which the electrons in the atoms are spinning. In most things, pairs of electrons in the atoms spin in opposite directions. Because of this, the magnetic fields they produce point in opposite directions, too. This makes the two magnetic fields cancel each other out—which is why most substances on Earth are not magnetic. In magnetic objects, however, some of the electron pairs spin in the same direction. Since the two magnetic fields produced by the electrons point in the same direction, they make one large magnetic field with double the strength.

In metals such as iron, steel, and cobalt, some of the electron pairs spin in the same direction. As a result, not all of the magnetic fields cancel out. The magnetic fields produced by the spinning electrons cause their atoms to line up. When this happens, the atoms produce small microscopic magnets called **magnetic domains.** In most pieces of iron or steel, the magnetic domains are pointing in different directions. When a piece of iron is brought in contact with a strong magnet, the magnet causes the

MAKING MAGNETS

Even though William Gilbert had no way of knowing what was going on inside a magnet, he discovered how to line up the magnetic domains in a piece of iron. Anyone can test this experiment. Take a steel paper clip and straighten it out. Rub a strong magnet against the paper clip again and again in the same direction. Make sure that you only rub in one direction. If you change direction you will scramble the magnetic domains. After about 50 passes with the magnet, touch the paper clip that you have been rubbing against another paper clip. A slight attraction should be possible to observe. The more you rub the clip with the magnet, the stronger the magnet will become.

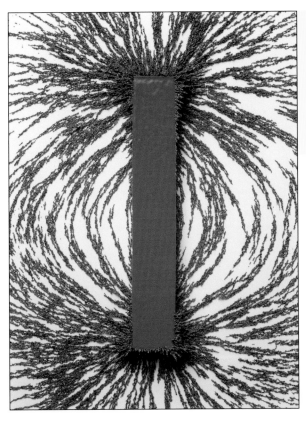

Tiny pieces of iron show the invisible lines of force surrounding this bar magnet. This allows you to see the size, shape, and direction of the magnetic field surrounding the magnet.

magnetic domains in the iron to point in the same direction. The piece of iron becomes a magnet.

Nature's Own Magnets

Using one magnet to make another magnet explains how some of them form, but you might be wondering where natural magnets come from. Lodestones get their magnetism from the earth. Lodestones are a kind of rock known as igneous rock, which forms from hot liquid rock called magma. As the magma cools, solid rock crystals form (similar to what happens when ice crystals form in freezing water, except at a much higher temperature, of course). Crystals with iron begin to form in the rock, and they line up with the magnetic field of Earth. When the rock—lodestone—has finally cooled, enough of the magnetic domains in the iron are pointing in the same direction to turn the rock into a magnet.

Electrons pass from the metal globe of the Van de Graaf generator into the person touching it and build up in his hair. Since these electrons all have a negative charge, the person's hair stands up because things with the same charge repel.

Static electricity is another force that was originally discovered by the ancient Greeks. The forces of magnets and static electricity work in the same way. When Gilbert was performing his investigations with magnets, he also experimented with static electricity.

Many people are already familiar with static electricity. For example, when a balloon is rubbed on someone's hair, the balloon will attract the hair. This happens because the same law of poles that works with magnets works with static electricity. Negatively charged electrons are removed from the hair and build up on the surface of the balloon as it is rubbed. The rubber in the balloon is actually removing some of the electrons from the hair. As a result, the balloon has extra negative charges. The hair, on the other hand, has lost some of its electrons, so now it has a positive charge. The two are now attracted to each other because they have opposite charges.

Gilbert had a hunch about this—the idea that static electricity and magnetism worked in the same way. But because he could see no obvious connection, he never could link the two. As it turns out, electricity and magnetism really are the same thing. It would take another 200 years for the connection to be made by a Danish schoolteacher experimenting with a new invention called the battery.

CHAPTER TWO

Current Electricity and Electromagnetism

I t's hard to imagine a world without electric power. It lights homes, cooks food, keeps houses and offices cool, and even entertains people. What some people may not realize, though, is that many of the modern marvels that are taken for granted today were thought of as science fiction 50 years ago. In fact, 200 years ago, even the simplest electrical devices such as lightbulbs didn't exist.

The story of modern electrical power and its connection to magnetism begins in the 1700s. Many scientists of the day, including Benjamin Franklin in the United States, Charles Du Fay in France, and Stephen Gray in England, were conducting experiments with static electricity. One of the most important discoveries during this time was how certain materials behaved around electric charges. **Conductors**, such as metals and salt water, allow electric charges to pass right through them. Other substances, such as rubber and glass, hold on to electric charges and stop them from moving on. These are called *insulators*.

Flipping Frog Legs

Static electricity inspired two scientists in Italy to investigate the connection between electricity and living things. Luigi Galvani was a teacher at the University of Bologna. One day, while dis-

Italian physicist Alessandro Volta is pictured with the world's first battery, known as the voltaic pile. Volta invented the battery in 1800 after a disagreement over the source of electricity with his contemporary, Italian physician Luigi Galvani.

secting a frog, Galvani noticed that its cut leg would twitch when it was brought near a machine that produced static electricity. In one famous experiment, Galvani took a frog's leg that he had dissected and hung it from a brass hook. When he placed the hook on an iron fence, the leg twitched. Galvani realized that electricity made the leg twitch. He believed that it was being produced in the body of the animal and published a paper describing his finding in 1791.

Alessandro Volta was a professor at Pavia University, who read Galvani's work but had another idea. Volta had also been studying static electricity. He repeated some of Galvani's experiments and concluded that the electricity was coming from another source. He suspected that the frog leg was simply reacting to the shock. Volta began experimenting with different metals and made a great discovery. When he took discs made of zinc and silver and connected them with pieces of felt that had been soaked in salt water, he was able to produce electricity. The electricity he produced with his device was different from static electricity, though. Volta produced the first type of **current electricity** and, in the process, also invented the first **battery.**

Go With the Flow

Current electricity is different from static electricity in several important ways. One is the way in which electrical charges are released from an object. Remember the balloon being rubbed on a person's hair? Here's another example of static electricity: When a person walks across a rug and touches a metal doorknob, he might feel a release, or discharge, of static electricity—a shock. Electrons are transferred from the rug to his body as he walks. When he gets near the metal knob (which is a conductor) the negatively charged electrons suddenly leap from his fingers. This is when he feels the shock. When there is a discharge of static electricity like this, all of the electrons move at the same time. This sudden motion isn't easy to control. With current electricity, however, electrons don't simply jump from one place to another.

THE BODY ELECTRIC

Volta was correct in his finding that the electricity in Galvani's experiment came from a source outside the frog's body. Yet, Galvani was right, too. It turns out that living things do produce their own electricity. In fact, the human body itself runs on it. Chemicals located in the cells of the body produce tiny electrical charges that run through the nerves. These charges help the brain regulate all body functions, including breathing and heart rate. When a person's heart stops beating, medical technicians often will use a device called an electric defibrillator to get the heart going again. The defibrillator gives the person an electric shock that "jump starts" the heart.

Instead, they flow steadily through a conductor, like water flowing through a pipe. Another way in which static electricity and current electricity differ is in the way they are produced. Rubbing two objects together produces static electricity, while current electricity can be produced through a chemical change in two different metals.

Battery Basics

Today, the technical name for the device that Volta built is an *electrochemical cell*, but most people simply call it a battery. A battery acts like a pump, pushing electrons through a wire, just as a pump pushes water through a pipe.

Pumps can move water using different amounts of pressure. Just like water pumps, different batteries use different amounts of pressure to pump electricity. The amount of electrical pressure in a battery is measured in **voltage**. The higher the voltage, the greater the push behind the flow of electrons. Most batteries have a label on them that describes their voltage. A typical flashlight battery is a D battery and has 1.5, or 1½, volts. AA, AAA, and C batteries have the same voltage as D batteries but they come in different sizes and shapes to fit into different devices. Most cars have 12-volt batteries in them. The small rectangular batteries that are common in many toys and portable electronic devices are 9-volt batteries.

Batteries produce **direct current,** or DC. This means that when the electrons flow, they all flow in the same direction. There is also another kind of electron flow, called **alternating current,** or AC. Alternating current is the kind of electricity that comes out of the wall outlets in a home or office.

Electromagnetism Reveals Itself

Before publicly revealing his discovery of current electricity, Volta conducted many different experiments to confirm his results. With each experiment, he found that whenever he brought two metals together with an acid, electric current would flow. In the year 1800, he described his findings in a letter to the Royal Society of London, the leading scientific organization in the world at that time. When his letter was read to the members of the society, it created quite a stir. Not only had Volta discovered a new type of electricity, but he also had invented a way of producing it in different amounts. Volta became an instant celebrity and received awards from many different governments and organizations.

Soon after Volta's discovery was announced, other scientists started experimenting with current electricity. In 1801 the English chemist Sir Humphry Davy found that he could make a simple electric light by using a powerful battery to create a spark between two rods of carbon. Davy was the head of the Royal Institution in London. With the help of his assistant Michael Faraday, he began investigating other uses of current electricity. Faraday would later build on this early work to make one of the most important discoveries connecting magnets and electricity. (Read on to find out what.)

England wasn't the only place where people were experimenting with current electricity. In 1819, a Danish schoolteacher named Hans Christian Øersted was also working with it. As the story goes, Øersted was doing a demonstration for one of his classes about how a battery worked, when he made a surprising discovery. He hooked up a wire to two ends of a battery and the

THE NAME GAME

The words *volt* and *voltage* both come from the name Volta. Once scientists began to understand the nature of electricity, they needed to create new terms to describe the properties of electrical current. The unit of electrical pressure was named after Volta to honor him for being the first person to discover electrical current. Luigi Galvani was remembered, too. The **galvanometer** was named after him. This is a device that measures the strength and direction of small amounts of electrical current.

In 1820, Danish physicist Hans Christian Øersted discovered a connection between electricity and magnetism, which is now known as electromagnetism. In this (*left*) engraving, Øersted is seen with his assistant as they demonstrate the effect of an electric current on a magnetic compass needle. The experiment was the first to ever show the relationship between electricity and magnetism.

current flowed through the wire. On the desk near the wire was a large magnetic compass. When Øersted moved the wire over the top of the compass, he found that the needle suddenly changed direction. When he moved the wire away again, the needle of the compass went back to its original position.

After the lecture Øersted continued to experiment with the battery, wire, and compass. He disconnected the wire from the battery and then reconnected it so that the wires were connected to the opposite ends of the battery. When he passed the wire over the compass, the needle moved again—only this time, it moved in the opposite direction. Somehow the current flowing through the wire was making the magnetic needle move. What

Øersted had discovered was the link between electricity and magnetism—**electromagnetism.**

Inside the Electromagnet

As was discussed earlier, magnets get their force from moving electrons. In iron and other magnetic materials, the spin of the electron produces a tiny magnetic field. If a large number of electrons began moving in the same direction, they would also produce a magnetic field. Since electrical current is really a flow of moving electrons, it makes sense that a wire carrying a current will also have a magnetic field around it. When the direction of the current is reversed, the direction of the magnetic field will reverse, too.

In a bar magnet, the magnetic field extends from the north pole to the south pole. The magnetic field in a wire carrying a current has a very different shape. Instead of extending from pole to pole, it wraps around the wire in little circles. If you were to take a wire and twist it into a loop, the magnetic field would become bunched together in the loop of wire. This makes the magnetic force stronger. The more loops that are in the wire, the stronger the magnetic field becomes.

Once news about Øersted's discovery got out, many other scientists started experimenting with the magnetic force created by wires carrying current electricity. In 1823, an English inventor

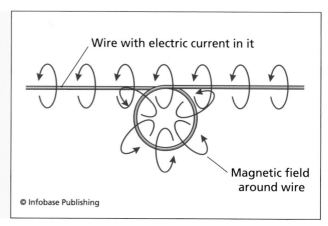

When an electric current flows through a wire, it produces a magnetic field that curves around the wire. When the wire is bent into a loop, the lines of force get bunched together and make the magnetic field stronger.

Wire with electric current in it

Magnetic field around wire

© Infobase Publishing

named William Sturgeon wrapped a copper wire 18 times around a horseshoe-shaped piece of iron. When he ran an electrical current through the wire, an amazing thing happened. The piece of iron acted like a magnet. As soon as he disconnected the wire from the battery, the magnetism in the iron stopped. Sturgeon had invented the first **electromagnet.**

Electromagnets are different from regular magnets in two important ways. A regular magnet is called a **permanent magnet**, because unless it's heated to very high temperatures, it will always be a magnet. An electromagnet is a **temporary magnet.** A temporary magnet is one that is only a magnet some of the time.

The second thing that makes an electromagnet different from a permanent magnet is its strength. You can control the strength of an electromagnet in two ways. The magnet becomes stronger as more coils of wire are wrapped around the metal conductor. The magnet will also become stronger when a larger current runs through the wire.

Both of the things that make electromagnets different from permanent magnets turned out to make this discovery extremely useful. The invention of the electromagnet gave people a new power source and a way to communicate over very long distances.

CHAPTER THREE

Magnets on the Move

When word of Øersted's discovery reached the Royal Institution in England, Sir Humphry Davy and several other scientists began searching for the cause of the magnetic force. At this time, people had no idea about the structure of the atom and had no clue that things like electrons even existed.

In 1821, Michael Faraday was asked to review Øersted's experiments and write up the findings for a scientific journal. Faraday was at this time the superintendent of the apparatus for the Royal Institution. In this post he had the use of the best scientific equipment in the world. Rather than just reporting on what others had done, Faraday decided to repeat all the experiments himself. He noticed something very interesting about Øersted's experiments. When a free-floating magnetic needle, like a compass, was brought near a current-carrying wire, the needle would spin in a circle. The only way he could explain this behavior was the idea that the magnetic field surrounding the wire was shaped like a circle. Faraday wrote up and published his findings, but few people understood the importance of what he had discovered.

Davy retired in 1825 and Faraday replaced him as the head of the Royal Institution. In his new position Faraday moved on to do other experiments dealing with chemistry. He would continue his

English chemist and physicist Michael Faraday is seen working in his laboratory at the Royal Institution of Great Britain. Faraday made great contributions to the fields of electromagnetism and electrochemistry, including his discovery of electromagnetic induction.

experiments with electromagnetism in 1831, but in the meantime a little-known schoolteacher in the United States named Joseph Henry was about to make the next big discovery.

While Faraday was working at the Royal Institution in London, Henry got a job at the Albany Academy in New York helping to conduct public science demonstrations. He began to take courses at the academy and eventually was able to get a job there teaching math and science. Henry set up a small lab and in 1826 began experimenting with electricity. He read about how William Sturgeon had built an electromagnet out of a coil of bare copper wire, an iron bar, and a battery. The magnet that Sturgeon made had a lifting power of about 7 pounds (3 kg). Henry started building his

A tangent galvanometer (*right*) is an instrument used to measure electric current. It was created to measure current after Hans Christian Øersted's 1820 discovery of the magnetic effect produced by electric currents.

own electromagnets. By wrapping larger and larger coils of wire around the iron core, he was able to make electromagnets that could lift more than 2,000 pounds (907 kg).

Making Electricity from Magnets

By 1829, Henry began to wonder if it was possible to use a magnet and a coil of wire to make electricity. It turned out that other scientists, including Faraday, had also asked this same question. Logically, it made sense. Since a coil of wire with electricity running through it made a magnet, it should be possible to reverse the process. Henry began experimenting and got the answer he was looking for by using a clever device. Instead of using a single coil of wire, he placed two wire coils next to each other. He hooked one wire on a galvanometer. He then attached the second coil to a battery. Both coils were insulated so they didn't touch each other. When he disconnected the coil from the battery, the galvanometer attached to the second coil moved. When he reconnected the wire, the galvanometer moved again.

As long as there was a steady flow of electrical current through the wire hooked up to the battery, there was no change in the galvanometer. Whenever the current changed strength or direction, the meter moved. This was because every time the current in the wire changed, the magnetic field around it also changed. Henry correctly reasoned that if a wire were placed in a changing magnetic field, the magnetic field would create an electrical current in the wire.

Rather than write up his results right away, Henry decided to keep experimenting to get more information. He put off publishing his discovery for more than two years. In May 1832, he got the shock of his life. While reading through the scientific journal *Proceedings of the Royal Institution*, he discovered that Faraday had made the same discovery in August 1831. Even though Henry had made the discovery first, the fact that Faraday published the results first meant that he is given credit for the discovery.

As it turned out, Faraday used an almost identical set of equipment as Henry. He then took it a step further, to remove all doubt that the electricity was coming from the magnet and not the battery. He took a coil of wire and attached it to a galvanometer. He then moved a permanent bar magnet in and out of the coil. Each time the magnet moved, the galvanometer showed that electricity was flowing through the wire. Since there were no batteries anywhere near the coil, the electricity had to be coming from the magnet. Because the magnet created, or *induced*, an electric current in the wire, the discovery became known as **electromagnetic induction**.

Electric Motors: Magnets Go Mobile

The discovery of electromagnetic induction was almost as important as Volta's discovery of current electricity itself. Using magnets and wire coils, people could now build devices to create electricity without using chemicals. Within 50 years, other inventors would use this discovery to power entire cities. Before that happened, though, both Faraday and Henry would make one more discovery that would get the world moving.

Before the year 1800, most factories were powered by water wheels. Water rushing down a river or stream would turn wheels located outside of a factory. The wheels were connected to devices inside the factory that powered its machinery. This of course meant that factories had to be located near sources of running water.

In the late 1700s, steam engines started replacing water wheels but they had several problems. For one thing, they were very noisy. Also, wood or coal boilers were needed to power steam engines, which meant they produced a great deal of smoke. But the biggest problem with steam engines was the fact that they frequently blew up if they weren't controlled properly.

MAY THE FORCE BE WITH YOU

One of the biggest challenges faced by scientists in the early 1800s was explaining why things such as electromagnetism happened. Back then, they knew very little about the structure of the atom, and the electron hadn't even been discovered yet. In order to explain why a magnet could make a current flow through a wire, Faraday came up with a brilliant idea involving forces. A force can be thought of as simply a push or a pull.

Recall that every magnet is surrounded by a magnetic field. This field can be made visible by spreading iron filings over the magnet. Faraday used this experiment to introduce the idea of a "force field." He said that the lines made by the iron filings showed where lines of force surrounded the magnet. He explained that when a wire moved past these lines of force, they would push the electricity through the wire. The faster the wire moved, or the more lines of force that it crossed, the more electricity would be made. If the wire stopped moving, no electricity would be made because no lines of force would be crossed. Without the lines of force to push the electricity through the wire, the current would not flow. Today, scientists call this **Faraday's Law**.

In their experiments with electromagnets, both Henry and Faraday discovered that it was possible to use an electromagnet and a permanent magnet together to create motion. Back in 1821, Faraday had noticed that a wire with an electric current flowing through it would move in a circle if it was brought near a permanent magnet. He used this discovery to create a simple electric motor.

Although Faraday's demonstration came first, it was Henry who really got the idea of an electric motor moving. Henry found that if he changed the direction of the electrical current in an electromagnet, the polarity of the magnet would switch. In other words, the end that had been the north pole would become the south pole. He reasoned that if he could keep switching the direction of the current in an electromagnet, he could make another magnet move back and forth. This was because the same poles would repel and the opposite poles would attract each other. In 1831 he built a simple device that caused an iron bar to rock back and forth as long as electrical current passed through it.

Motors Go Mainstream

Although most people saw Henry's invention as simply being a toy, a few inventors took notice and began to improve on it. By the end of the 1800s, electric motors had replaced many steam engines in factories. Not only were they quieter and less dangerous to operate, but also they could be made in different sizes depending on the job they needed to do. The biggest advantage was that electric motors were clean because they did not have to burn a fuel. To start and stop one, all you had to do was flip a switch.

Instead of rocking back and forth, modern electric motors spin, just like a water wheel. The simplest form of a motor uses a ring of magnets called a **stator** and a metal shaft with a coil of wire wrapped around it called the **rotor**. The rotor sits in a cradle between the two poles of the stator. When a current is put into the coil, it causes it to become a magnet. The poles in the rotor inter-

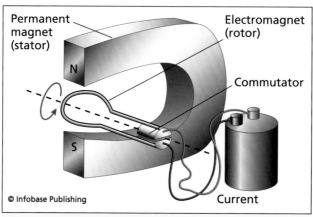

Permanent magnet (stator)

N

S

Electromagnet (rotor)

Commutator

Current

© Infobase Publishing

The simplest type of electric motor has two main parts. On the outside is a permanent horseshoe magnet called the stator. Between the poles of the stator is a loop of wire through which electric current flows. This is called the rotor. When electricity flows through the rotor, it becomes an electromagnet. The poles of the rotor interact with the poles of the stator, making the motor turn. In order to keep the motor spinning, a device called a commutator changes the direction of current flow every half turn in the rotor. This way, the similar poles of the two magnets are always near each other and they repel, which makes the motor turn.

act with the poles in the stator. As they attract and repel each other, the rotor spins. To keep the rotor spinning, a device called a **commutator** causes the current direction in the rotor to reverse with every half turn.

Getting Power to the People

In 1831 Faraday proved that a magnet could be used to make an electric current flow through a wire. Demonstrating magnetic induction was the easy part. Turning the idea into a useful device was difficult. In order to keep the electricity flowing in the wire, he would have to create a device in which some kind of conductor would keep cutting across the magnetic **lines of force**. After two months of experimenting, Faraday solved the problem.

First he created a magnetic field with a large, U-shaped magnet. Between the poles of the magnet he set up a large copper disc that had a metal rod, or shaft, going through the middle of it. The shaft was attached to a crank. When the crank was turned, the disc turned, cutting through the lines of force created by the magnet. When he attached wire brushes to the edge of the copper disc and the metal shaft, electricity flowed through the wire. As long as the disc turned, he was able to generate a current. Faraday had built the world's first **electric generator**.

The invention of the generator opened the door for the electrical industry. Until that time, the only way people could produce electrical current was with batteries. Batteries produce electricity using a chemical reaction. As the chemicals inside a battery get used up, though, batteries grow weak and eventually stop working. This means they must be replaced fairly often. In order to generate a great deal of electrical energy, many batteries need to be connected, which becomes very expensive.

Once people had generators, all they needed to do to keep the current flowing was to keep the generator turning. This could be done using a water wheel, a steam engine, or even a hand crank. If a job needed more electrical power, it had to have a bigger coil that turned faster. Soon after Faraday built his first generator, inventors all over Europe and the United States began constructing devices of their own. This led to many different improvements. It also led to one big complication that would soon after lead to a battle between two of the greatest industrial giants of the nineteenth century.

The Current Wars: AC versus DC

All batteries have two ends, which are called terminals. One terminal is labeled negative (–) and the other is labeled positive (+). When you connect a device to a battery,

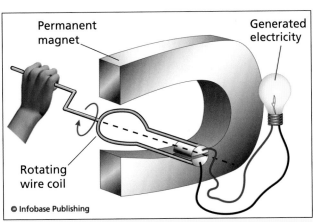

An electric **generator** is really the same thing as an electric motor, but turned backward. In a motor, an electrical current is put into the rotor coil, which causes it to spin. In a generator, some type of mechanical device such as a hand crank or wheel is what turns the rotor, and electrical current is produced.

the electricity flows out of the negative terminal, through the device and back into the battery at the positive terminal. This continuous loop is called a **circuit**. Since all the electrons are flowing in one direction, the type of current is called DC, for direct current. Simple generators produce alternating current, or AC. In an alternating current circuit, electrons do not flow in one direction. Instead, they vibrate back and forth. As they vibrate, they set off a chain reaction in which one electron bangs into the next. This is what makes the current flow.

In the 1850s, inventors in England and the United States began experimenting with a new type of electric light. They were called incandescent lamps, and used a small wire called a filament to produce the light. The filaments in early incandescent lamps got too hot too quickly, and as a result burnt out after only a short time. Because of this, they were not very useful.

One of the most famous people to tackle the problem was an American inventor and businessman, Thomas Alva Edison. He had already made a name for himself inventing many different devices, including the stock market ticker and the phonograph. He was an extremely devoted inventor, and wanted to spend even more of his time and effort to invent other useful things. In particular, he became obsessed in the quest to invent a long-lasting electric lightbulb. Edison set up a laboratory in Menlo Park, New Jersey, which he called his "invention factory," and hired the best assistants he could find. So many different inventions came from his lab that the newspapers started calling Edison the "Wizard of Menlo Park."

After working on the problem for more than two years, Edison and his helpers came up with a way to make the filament last longer. By 1879 they perfected the first practical electric lightbulb. The problem was that, at this time, most people did not have electricity in their homes. Before Edison could sell his electric lights, he had to invent a whole system to distribute electrical power to the people.

Thomas Alva Edison is photographed holding a light bulb. Although Edison did not invent the electric light, he improved upon the idea and created a practical, long-lasting light as well as an electrical lighting system that provided a way to mass-distribute electricity.

He started big—in nearby New York City. He began by first building a power plant in Manhattan to generate electricity. His assistants designed sockets and switches that were used to connect lights in people's homes to electrical circuits. Everything seemed to be set—until it was discovered that there was a problem with the power.

When Edison had designed his system, he built everything to work with DC, because direct current was simpler to work with. The big problem with DC, however, is that it is difficult to send over a long distance. To do so, an extremely thick wire is needed, which makes the electricity very expensive to transport. Edison had a hard time sending his DC power more than a mile (1.5 km) from the generator. If he were to electrify a large city, he would need to build a separate power plant every few miles.

Although some devices needed DC, electrical lights worked just as well with alternating current. Since many generators made alternating current to start with, AC could be used to power lights directly. Most importantly, unlike direct current, AC could be transported over long distances without having to use thick conducting wires. AC seemed to be the logical solution to the problem.

While Edison was trying to work out the problems with a system to distribute direct current power, another inventor named George Westinghouse was putting his money behind AC. Like Edison, Westinghouse was a self-made man. Early on he learned how to use different types of machinery and loved to invent. By 1869, he had developed a new braking system for trains, and within a few years, most of the passenger trains in the United States were equipped with Westinghouse safety brakes. Young Westinghouse became a wealthy man.

Like Edison, Westinghouse was interested in many different areas of science and would go on to patent more than 100 inventions. While traveling in Europe, he saw how alternating current was being used there to power factories. Westinghouse thought that by using this technology, he could develop a system for powering entire cities. He set up a small power station using AC current in Pittsburgh, Pennsylvania, and hired some of the best electrical engineers he could find to run it. In 1886 he set up the Westinghouse Electric and Manufacturing Company.

Westinghouse's AC system quickly proved to be more efficient and less costly than Edison's DC system. To make matters worse for Edison, Westinghouse purchased the rights to a new AC electric motor that had been developed by a brilliant young scientist named Nikola Tesla. By using Tesla's motors, AC could now be used to power machines in factories. Tesla went to work for Westinghouse to improve the generators.

While Edison was still regarded as the world's leading expert on electricity, his company was quickly losing to Westinghouse. In order to slow the growth of AC systems, Edison's supporters played up the idea that alternating current was much more dangerous than direct current. They planted stories in the newspapers about people who had supposedly been killed by AC. They even went as far as to hold public demonstrations of the dangers of AC by electrocuting stray animals. Westinghouse fought back and the battle became known as "the current wars."

Despite this negative publicity, AC power proved to be better and Westinghouse continued to win major contracts to build power systems. In 1893, his system was selected to power the World's Columbian Exposition. Later, using Tesla's improved AC generators, he set up the first hydroelectric generating system tapping the power of Niagara Falls. Today, almost all the electricity that powers homes, schools, and factories is AC. Despite being known as the wizard of Menlo Park, Edison lost the current war.

CHAPTER FOUR

Communicating with Electromagnets

Before the mid 1800s, the only way that people could communicate over very long distances was by letters or messages carried on foot, horseback, or railroad. The problem with sending messages this way was that it took a great deal of time—time to write the message, time to transport it, and then more time waiting for an answer. To send a message hundreds of miles could take days, and if it were going across the ocean, a person could wait months for a reply. What the world needed was a way for people to communicate instantaneously across the country or across an ocean, as easily as speaking to someone across the room. Electromagnetism made that possible.

The Electromagnetic Telegraph

The word *telegraph* basically means "sending a message over a distance." Using the discoveries of Henry and Faraday, several inventors came up with simple electromagnetic devices that could get the job done. In England in 1837, William Cooke and Charles Wheatstone made the first working electric **telegraph** system. The way it worked was quite simple. A circuit was set up

Cooke and Wheatstone's electric telegraph was patented in 1837. British physicists William Cooke and Charles Fothergill Wheatstone applied electromagnetic devices to power their telegraph. The electric telegraph was a breakthrough for modern communication.

with a needle at one end and a switch at the other. The person who was sending the message would close the switch and electricity would flow through the circuit. This would turn on an electromagnet at the **receiver**'s end that would make a needle move and point to a letter.

In order to be able to point to all 26 letters of the alphabet, the original Cooke and Wheatstone telegraph used six lines of wire with five different needles at the receiving end. To send messages back, the person at the receiving end would use an entirely separate system. All of this was very difficult to operate, very slow, and quite expensive to build. By 1842, Cooke and Wheatstone had designed a receiver with only two needles, but it was still slow and expensive. Even with all the problems, however, it was a major breakthrough. By 1852 more than 4,000 miles (6,400 km) of telegraph lines were strung in England.

Mr. Morse Invents a Code

While Cooke and Wheatstone were working in England, Samuel F. B. Morse was making a name for himself with his own telegraph system in the United States. Morse was an artist by trade and had very little background in science. He became interested in the idea of long-distance communication in 1832 while he was sailing back to his country from England. On board the ship, he learned about the discovery of the electromagnet and the work of Faraday. As he read about the discoveries, he reasoned that he could use an electromagnet to set up a simple signaling device. By the time he reached the United States, he had drawn up the plans for his system.

He began working on the idea and by 1837 had a model of a simple telegraph. In this system, the sender would press a key that sent electricity to an electromagnet at the other end of a circuit. The magnet would control the movement of a strip of paper

THE TELEGRAPH PROVES ITS USEFULNESS

In 1845, the telegraph proved its worth by helping to catch a criminal in England. A murder suspect was seen getting on a train as it was pulling out of the Paddington station. An alert station manager telegraphed the station manager in the town of Slough, several miles away. The Slough station manager contacted the police. When the train arrived at the station, the police were waiting and the suspect was captured.

As batteries and relays improved, telegraph systems covered longer and longer distances. In 1851, a telegraph cable was run under the English Channel connecting England and France. Seven years later, a similar cable was laid under the Atlantic Ocean. Once the system was activated, the time it took to send a message from New York to London was cut from more than a month to just a few minutes.

Between 1850 and 1870, the Post Office Telegraph Service used this early Morse key. The Morse key was a device used to send long-distance written messages by transmitting electric currents that were converted into sounds, and then manually converted into letters by a skilled operator.

at the other end. A pen would mark the paper. If the operator held the key down for a long time, the pen would make a dash. A quick press of the key would make a dot. Using a combination of dots and dashes, Morse came up with a code for every letter in the alphabet. Morse code was one of the first real digital systems, because using only two symbols it could spell out an unlimited number of words. Even with all of today's advances in communication, most radio operators still must learn Morse code.

Morse Code Decoded

The paper-tape system that Morse first came up with wasn't very practical. Enlisting the help of an assistant who had a better knowledge of science, he changed his system to use a *sounder*. This device had an electromagnet that made a key click when a key at the other end of the circuit was pressed. The system was a great success because instead of many needles and wires, it only used one wire. The new system still used Morse code, but instead of having dots and dashes written on paper, the operator would listen for the pauses between clicks. A short pause was a dot and a long pause was a dash.

Even with these improvements, the telegraph still had one major problem. Each telegraph system had its own circuit, which ran on a single battery. It could only send a message for a few miles before the signal got too weak. To get around the problem, operators would relay the message from one town to the next, but this took time.

The big breakthrough came when Morse presented his problem to Joseph Henry. By this time Henry was a professor at Princeton University in New Jersey. Several years earlier, Henry had come up with a device called a relay. The relay had a horseshoe-shaped electromagnet, which connected directly to the circuit in place of the sounder. When the electrical signal came from the sender's key, it would trigger a magnet on the relay. The relay was connected to another circuit with its own battery. This second circuit would then automatically send the signal to another relay, until the message finally reached the destination.

Using this new system, Morse set up a telegraph line from Washington, D.C., to Baltimore, Maryland, a distance of about 40 miles (64 km). On May 24, 1844, he tested the system by sending the message "What hath God wrought?" This was only the first of many long-distance messages to be sent using his telegraph and code.

Calling Mr. Bell

Even though new lines were springing up all over the world, the telegraph was still not an ideal way to communicate. Telegraphs required trained operators to send the messages. There was no such thing as a private telegraph message. What people really wanted was a device that they could use without another person being involved. When a young inventor named Alexander Graham Bell designed the first telephone, the way the world communicated took a giant leap forward.

Bell was born in Edinburgh, Scotland, in 1847. His father, Alexander Melville Bell, was an expert on speech and hearing. In 1870 the family moved from Scotland to Canada. In 1871, Bell traveled to the United States and began teaching at the Boston School for the Deaf. By this time, the telegraph had seen many improvements, but there was still one big problem: only one message at a time could be sent over a wire. The challenge for inventors was to come up with a way of sending several messages simultaneously over the same wire. While in Boston, Bell heard about the problem and thought he had the answer.

Using his understanding of the way sound travels, Bell came up with the idea of making a "harmonic telegraph." In this system, several different messages could be sent over a single wire at the same time using a set of tuning forks. The idea was a good one, but building the system was much too complicated for Bell to do alone. Fortunately, he met a talented model builder named Thomas Watson, and the two of them turned out to be a perfect match. By June 1875, Bell and Watson had worked out most of the details of sending sound using a set of vibrating metal reeds instead of forks. Each reed was attached to a coil of an electromagnet.

Alexander Graham Bell designed a candlestick telephone (*above*) in 1878. Although many people, including Italian inventor Antonio Meucci, claim to have invented the telephone, Bell was granted the U.S. patent for the invention of the telephone in 1876.

One of the reeds became stuck during one of their tests. While Watson worked to free it, Bell, who was in the other room, heard sound come through the receiver. The stuck reed was actually picking up the sounds in the room. The two men quickly realized that this same type of system could be used to transmit an actual voice. They gave up on the harmonic telegraph and on March 7, 1876, Bell was given the credit for making the world's first telephone.

The Technology of the Telephone

The main difference between the telephone and the telegraph is the way in which the electrical current is sent through the wire. In a telegraph, the electric current is started and stopped by the telegraph key, which acts like a switch. In a telephone, the current flows continuously through the wire; it is the strength, or intensity, of the current that changes. What Bell and Watson discovered was a way to change the intensity of the current, just as a person can change the loudness of his voice as he speaks.

The earliest telephone had a separate receiver and **transmitter**. The transmitter had a thin metal disc, which was placed over a coil of wire wrapped around a magnetic iron core. When a person spoke into the transmitter, the thin metal disk moved up and down, causing the coil to move back and forth past the magnet. This motion created a small electrical current that would follow the pattern of the person's voice. The current was made stronger using a battery, and it then traveled through a wire to a receiver. The receiver was basically the transmitter in reverse. The incoming current would cause a magnetic coil to move back and forth. The coil was attached to a larger metal disk, which vibrated and reproduced the sound of the person's voice.

Strange Attractions

The sound quality of the first telephones was not very good. During the years following its invention, Bell and other inventors made many changes in the way the transmitter and receiver worked. Some of the biggest improvements came from Thomas Edison, who had also solved the problem of sending multiple messages over a telegraph line. By the late 1800s, telephone and telegraph lines were crisscrossing the country.

As telegraph systems became bigger and the current they carried got stronger, linemen (the people who worked on the telegraph and telephone lines) began to notice something interesting. Many of the iron hooks and nails near the telegraph lines were becoming magnetized. This would have been easy to explain if the current-carrying wires were actually touching the metal. But the magnetized metal was often some distance away from the wires. It was almost as if the wires were magnetizing the metal through thin air. These observations did not fit into any of the scientific theories of the time, and even men like Joseph Henry and Michael Faraday couldn't explain it.

After working for several years to solve this mystery, a Scottish scientist named James Clerk Maxwell finally made sense of it. Not only did he explain how magnetism could move through the air, but also he completely changed what people thought about the way light travels. Maxwell's discoveries led other inventors to develop even more devices using electromagnetism, from the first radios to X-rays and beyond.

CHAPTER FIVE

The Electromagnetic Spectrum

James Clerk Maxwell loved science and was a whiz in math. As a student at Cambridge University, Maxwell read about Faraday's discoveries and was particularly interested in the concept that a magnet was surrounded by lines of force. Rather than simply experimenting with lines of force, Maxwell began to put together mathematical explanations of how they worked. Starting in 1861, he wrote several papers discussing his new ideas. After three years of work he was finally able to present all his models in one neat package.

The paper was called "A Dynamical Theory of the Electromagnetic Field." In it he presented a series of four mathematical equations that tied together electricity and magnetism. Instead of treating them as separate forces, he showed them to be two parts of the same force. The new force was simply called the **electromagnetic field.**

In the paper, Maxwell explained that electromagnetic force moved away from an electrically charged object in wave-like movements, and at the speed of light. This explained how iron

When a rock splashes into a pond, waves move across the water, starting from the place where the rock hit. Waves are produced whenever something is moved. The rock hitting the pond pushes some of the water out of the way. That water then pushes more water in a chain reaction. Electromagnetic waves form in the same way, except that instead of water being pushed, the disturbance takes place in an electromagnetic field. When an electric current flows through a wire, it causes a change in the magnetic field around the wire. This change doesn't stop with the first field. It moves across space in a series of electromagnetic pulses, or waves.

objects near telegraph lines could become magnetized. As a current flowed through the telegraph wire, it created an electromagnetic field around the wire. The field moved out from the wire in **electromagnetic waves**. When the waves hit a piece of iron, they magnetized the metal.

Because the waves traveled at the speed of light, Maxwell also suggested that light itself was related to electromagnetism. He discovered that both light and heat are forms of electromagnetic energy, which travel in waves across space. He also suggested that there could be other forms of **radiation** that had not been discovered yet. This proved to be one of the greatest predictions in science. In less than 50 years, other scientists would discover other forms of electromagnetic energy, such as **radio waves**, **X-rays**, and gamma rays. All these forms of radiation are caused by electromagnetic waves moving through space.

The easiest way to understand wave motion is to examine the parts of a wave. Every wave has a high point and a low point. The high point is called the *crest*, and the low point is the *trough*. The *amplitude* describes the height of the wave from its midpoint to the top of the crest. The more energy used, the greater the displacement and the bigger the amplitude of the wave. The distance from one wave crest to the next is called the **wavelength**.

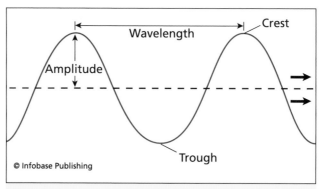

This is a sine wave. A wave has three main parts. The top of the wave is called the crest and the bottom of the wave is the trough. One wavelength is the distance from one crest to the next crest (or one trough to the next trough). The height of the wave is the amplitude. It is measured from the middle of the wave to either the top of a crest or the bottom of a trough.

Long waves are very spread out, while the crests of short waves are bunched close together.

When waves are produced, there is usually not just one wave, but many waves moving out in a row. Think of a ringing bell. When the bell rings, it shakes back and forth, or **vibrates**. Each vibration will cause a new sound wave to form. The speed at which waves are created is called the **frequency.** The faster something vibrates, the greater the frequency of the waves it creates.

The Electromagnetic Spectrum

The colored bands of a rainbow make what scientists call a **spectrum.** Back in the late 1600s, scientist and philosopher Isaac Newton used a triangular piece of glass to create a spectrum of sunlight. What he proved was that white light (the light from the sun or a lamp) is really a blend of many different colors. One end of the spectrum is red and the other is violet. In between are orange, yellow, green, and blue. When white light hit the piece of glass and split up into the spectrum, he found that the spectrum always had the same pattern of colors in the same order.

Although Newton's discovery was a major breakthrough, he couldn't explain why it happened. Maxwell's work with electromagnetic waves provided the answer. Light travels in waves, and each color of light has its own special wavelength. In addition, the waves for each color of light vibrate at different rates, or frequencies. Red light has the longest wavelength and vibrates the slowest. Violet light has the shortest wavelength and vibrates the fastest. There are other forms of electromagnetic radiation that are not visible to the human eye, but can be detected by using special tools.

A Full Spectrum of Waves

Visible light (the light our eyes can see) makes up only a tiny part of a much bigger group of electromagnetic waves called the **electromagnetic spectrum.** At one end of the spectrum are radio waves. These waves vibrate the slowest and have very long wavelengths. At the other end of the spectrum are extremely high-energy waves called gamma rays. When gamma waves travel, they vibrate at speeds of more than one million trillion times per second. Visible light is near the middle of the electromagnetic spectrum.

Directly below visible light on the spectrum are infrared waves. Although infrared waves cannot be seen, they can be felt. They are commonly called heat waves. When satellites take pictures of Earth, they often use infrared cameras to show where "hot spots" are. These images allow scientists to track changes in patterns of how land is used, and even to see warm and cold currents in the ocean. Night vision goggles also depend upon infrared rays, as does the remote control for a television.

Directly above the visible light part of the spectrum is ultraviolet, or UV radiation. Even though human eyes can't detect it, human skin can. Ultraviolet light is the part of the spectrum that causes sunburn if a person is not protected by sunscreen.

Heinrich Hertz Broadcasts Radio Waves

Once Maxwell's equations were published, scientists all over the world tried to prove that electromagnetic waves really existed. Many thought that Maxwell was totally wrong, but others put together clever experiments to test the theory. One of these scientists was a German named Heinrich Rudolf Hertz.

Hertz was born in 1857 in Hamburg, Germany. As a young man, he attended the University of Berlin and studied under the brilliant scientist Herman von Helmholtz, a world authority on energy and electromagnetic fields. Helmholtz taught Hertz well. Hertz graduated in 1880, and in 1883 began to work on proving Maxwell's theory of electromagnetic waves.

The breakthrough came four years later. Hertz constructed a device with two large metal balls separated by a small gap. He attached a wire to the balls and produced an electrical spark between them with a high-voltage alternating current (AC). On the other side of the room, he fashioned a second device from a

German physicist Heinrich Hertz was the first to successfully prove that electricity can be transmitted in electromagnetic waves. His discovery would later lead to the invention of the wireless telegraph, radio, and television.

loop of wire with another small gap in it. Whenever he turned on the current in the first device, a spark would appear in the gap of the wire loop. The only way that the electricity could have moved from the first device to the second was through the air. Hertz had proved that electromagnetic waves were real.

During the few months that followed, Hertz was able to construct devices that would send electromagnetic waves farther than 60 feet (18 meters). The device that made the first electric spark came to be known as a transmitter because it sent, or transmitted, the waves out into space. The device with the wire loop was called the receiver because it picked up, or received, the wave. Because these waves moved out, or *radiated,* in all directions, they later became known as *radio waves.* Over time, other scientists found that by changing the size and the shape of the wire loop, they could pick up more of these waves. This gave rise to the idea of an **antenna.**

Mr. Marconi Invents Wireless

Following Hertz's demonstration, other scientists made improvements to both the transmitter and receiver that allowed radio waves to be broadcast over greater distances. It took a young man from Italy to really see radio's potential use. Guglielmo Marconi was born in Bologna, Italy, in 1874. Marconi's family was quite wealthy, so he didn't have to worry about learning a trade such as carpentry or metalwork. He was interested in science, though, and it was while studying physics that he read about the discoveries of Maxwell and Hertz.

The idea of sending invisible waves through the air fascinated Marconi, who began experimenting on his own. By the age of 20 Marconi realized that these new waves could actually be used to send telegraph messages without the use of wires. In less than a year, he had built a system that could send and receive radio waves over a distance of almost two miles (3 km).

Marconi could not interest anyone in Italy in his new wireless system, so he moved to England. With the support of the English

Italian Guglielmo Marconi invented wireless telegraphy, or radio, as we know it today. He was the first to send wireless signals across the Atlantic Ocean.

postal service manager, Marconi was able to improve his equipment. By 1899 he was sending wireless telegraph messages across the English Channel and then across the Atlantic Ocean. Very soon after, ship owners began installing these new systems on their vessels.

Even though he was not trained as a scientist, Marconi won the 1909 Nobel Prize in Physics for his work on the wireless telegraph. In 1912, a wireless operator using a Marconi system aboard the ocean liner *Titanic* sent out a distress signal to other ships in the area after it hit an iceberg. Although more than 1,500 people died in the accident, hundreds of others were saved because rescue ships picked up the message and were able to reach the survivors.

Radio Broadcasts for the Masses
When Marconi first developed his wireless system, its main use was to send messages using Morse code. As more scientists and

inventors worked with the system, however, they discovered that wireless could do other things. In 1904, an English scientist named John Ambrose Fleming developed a special tube that controlled the flow of electrons in a circuit. This device was called a Fleming valve. It greatly increased the power of radio receivers and allowed them to make a signal louder. On Christmas Eve, 1906, Reginald Aubrey Fessenden connected a microphone from a telephone to his wireless system. By using the microphone to control the signal, he was able to transmit his own voice over the air. This was the first known radio broadcast.

During World War I, inventors made many more improvements in radio systems. After the war, a number of different companies, including Westinghouse and the Radio Corporation of

GENERAL SARNOFF LEADS THE BROADCASTING CHARGE

Even though he wasn't a scientist or an inventor, few people did as much to promote radio and television broadcasting as David Sarnoff. Born in Russia in 1891, Sarnoff moved to the United States in 1900. As luck would have it, he wound up getting a job as the personal messenger to Guglielmo Marconi, who had come to the United States to set up his wireless systems.

Sarnoff learned how to be a wireless operator and quickly rose in the ranks of the American Marconi Company. In 1916 he pushed for the company to start building "radio music boxes" and make broadcasts of music, news, and other popular programming. In 1921 he became general manager of the newly formed Radio Corporation of America, and five years later, he formed the National Broadcasting Company (NBC).

In the early 1930s, Sarnoff hired Russian scientist Alexander Zworykin to help develop television, and NBC made the first successful TV broadcast in 1939. During World War II, Sarnoff used his talents to bring together all the radio communication systems in England, the United States, and the other countries in the group known as the Allies. For his efforts, he was promoted to the rank of general.

America (RCA), started thinking about offering regular broadcasts of news and entertainment. On November 2, 1920, the United States's first radio station business, KDKA, went "on the air" from the top of the Westinghouse building in Pittsburgh, Pennsylvania. Only two years later, there were 564 official broadcasting stations operating in the United States. During the first half of the twentieth century, radio broadcasts ruled the air. This all changed in 1939, however, when NBC broadcast the first television pictures from the World's Fair to viewers in New York City—only a hint of some of the magnificent electromagnetic marvels that would be developed through the following 70 years.

CHAPTER SIX

Modern Electromagnetic Marvels

These days, radio waves are necessary for much more than communication and entertainment. When used in a **radar** system, they help air traffic controllers keep track of planes, meteorologists follow dangerous storms, and police catch drivers traveling at unsafe speeds. The term radar is an acronym: it stands for **ra**dio **d**etection **a**nd **r**anging. British scientists who were trying to come up with an early warning system against air attacks from Germany during World War II developed the first radar systems back in the 1930s.

The idea behind radar is really quite simple. It's based on the same principle that causes an echo. The most basic radar system sends a short burst of high-energy radio waves in a set direction. When the waves strike a distant object, they bounce off and return to the spot from which they first left and are picked up by a radar receiver. Since radio waves travel at the speed of light, the operator can calculate the distance to the object by measuring how much time it takes for the reflected wave to return.

The idea of using radio waves to detect distant objects started popping up almost as soon as radio waves were discovered. In 1900, Nikola Tesla came up with a plan to use reflected radio waves to track moving ships at sea. Based on some of Tesla's experiments using high-voltage electricity, the British Air Ministry began investigating the possibility of using radio waves as a "death ray" for shooting down enemy planes.

Radar Really Gets Cooking

By 1939 experiments proved that a reliable radar tracking system could be built. As World War II began, the British government quickly constructed a line of radar towers along the English Channel. During the war these stations were able to give the Royal Air Force advance warning of approaching German planes. This enabled them to ready their fighter planes and prepare for the attack. Radar also saved the lives of countless citizens because the advanced warning gave them enough time to get to bomb shelters where they were safe from attack.

One of the people who helped make radar practical was an electronic genius named Percy L. Spencer. He worked for the Raytheon Company, which specialized in making radar systems. After the war, Raytheon continued to make radar systems for uses during times of peace. One day in 1946, Spencer was working on a new and improved **magnetron**, which is at the heart of the radar system. This device uses an electromagnetic field to produce radio waves called **microwaves**.

While he was working on his project, Spencer got an interesting surprise. According to the story, when he stepped in front of the magnetron, a chocolate bar in his shirt pocket started to melt. Although most people would have been worried about washing the melted candy out of their clothes, Spencer was more interested in why the candy melted. What he discovered was that the microwave radiation coming out of the magnetron caused nearby objects to heat up.

After a few more months of experimenting with the magnetron and other types of food, Spencer was convinced that he could turn his accidental discovery into a new product. By 1953 he had created the first "high frequency dielectric heating apparatus." To

During World War II, the British government used a radar system as a preventive measure against approaching German fighter planes. The radar stations gave the British Army advanced knowledge of the enemy's location, which allowed time to prepare for the attack and get innocent citizens to safety. Radar towers, like the one at left, gathered the signals from great distances.

the delight of popcorn lovers all over the world, the microwave oven was born.

Medical Marvels

With so many scientists working all over the world with electromagnetism, it is not surprising that the force has come to be used for many different needs. While Maxwell and Hertz were doing the first experiments with electromagnetic waves, other scientists were testing the effects of high-voltage electricity. Using sealed glass tubes with a metal plate at each end, they were able to pass electrical currents through a vacuum. When this happened, rays flowed from the negatively charged end (called the cathode) to the positively charged end of the tube. Whenever these rays—called *cathode rays*—were produced, the tube glowed. What was even more amazing was that when a magnetic field was brought near the cathode rays, the beam would bend.

In 1895, a German scientist named Wilhelm Röntgen was experimenting with one of these tubes. The room was completely dark, and on the other side of the room was a piece of special paper used to print photographs. Whenever he turned on the tube, the photographic paper began to glow. Röntgen continued to experiment with the tube and found that even when he put different materials, such as wood or aluminum, in front of the paper, it still glowed every time the tube was turned on. He became convinced that the tube was producing another type of invisible radiation. Because these mysterious rays could not be seen, he called them X-rays.

During the next year, Röntgen was able to use the tube to focus X-rays in different directions. In one of his most famous experiments, he had his wife place her hand on top of a photographic film plate. He then shot a beam of X-rays through her hand and onto the film plate. When he developed the film, he was amazed to find that the X-rays had gone right through her skin and produced a perfect image of her bones on the plate.

PICTURE THIS

The tube that Röntgen used in his experiments is called a cathode ray tube, or CRT. Today, cathode ray tubes are used for more than science experiments. The CRT is at the heart of most television picture tubes, computer monitors, and displays for all sorts of electronic devices. Modern CRTs have a fluorescent screen at one end and an electron gun at the other end. The electron gun shoots a beam of electrons at the screen, which makes the screen glow. Magnetic plates in the middle of the tube are used to bend the beam of electrons. This allows the beam to produce an image.

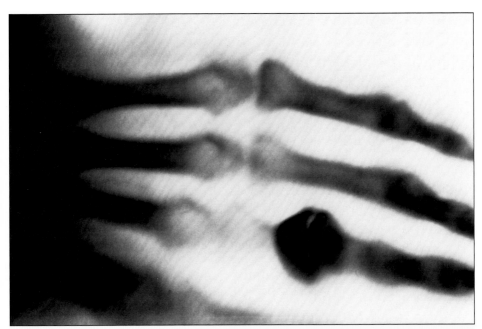

The first visible image of bones inside the body is the famous 1895 X-ray photograph of German scientist Wilhelm Röntgen's wife's hand (*above*). Röntgen was experimenting with cathode rays when he made the discovery of X-rays, which were able to pass through matter. Röntgen was awarded the first-ever Noble Prize in Physics in 1901.

It is now known that X-rays are really just another form of electromagnetic radiation with a wavelength that is shorter than visible light. X-ray machines today basically work in the same way as the system that Röntgen first built. Even so, during the last 50 years, advances in medical technology have been truly amazing. Röntgen's discovery is now more that just an interesting thing to play with—it's an extremely important medical tool. In the past, when a doctor wanted to know what was going on inside of a person's body, the only option was to cut the patient open and look inside.

One of the problems with a basic X-ray, however, is that it only produces a flat image from one direction. By combining computer technology with X-rays, though, doctors can make a 3-D picture of both bones and muscle. This is called a **computerized**

axial tomography (CAT) scan. The CAT scanner still uses X-rays, but instead of a beam from one direction, the X-rays approach a target (such as a person's head) from many angles. Using CAT scans, doctors can locate such problems as tumors and blood clots, which would not show up on a regular X-ray.

X-ray machines and CAT scanners have indeed helped doctors a great deal, but they both still have their limits. They work best on dense materials like bones and tumors. To see what's going on in soft tissues, the new device of choice is the **magnetic resonance imager** or **MRI**. American scientists Felix Bloch and Edward Purcell developed the principles behind it in 1945.

An MRI scan begins with the patient going inside a giant circular ring of extremely powerful electromagnets. When the electromagnets are turned on, the hydrogen atoms in the person's body begin to align with the magnetic field that the electromagnets make. Next, the patient is hit with a beam of radio waves from a different direction. This causes the nuclei of the hydrogen atoms to vibrate. When the radio waves are turned off, the nuclei relax and go back to their original positions.

As the nuclei give back the energy they gained from the radio waves, they do so at different rates. The intensity of this energy is picked up by a coil, which sends it into a computer. The computer then uses the differences in energy intensity to make a map of the area of the person's body being studied. Using an

---

MAGNETIC COWS?

One type of extremely powerful magnet is called a "cow magnet." It is made from a special alloy called "AlNiCo," which stands for aluminum, nickel, and cobalt. Farmers feed these magnets to their cows. A cow has four stomach chambers, and after the cow swallows the magnet, it sits in the first of these chambers. If the cow accidentally eats small pieces of steel wire and nails, the metal is attracted to the magnet. This keeps the tiny bits of metal from passing through the cow's intestines, which could cause severe damage.

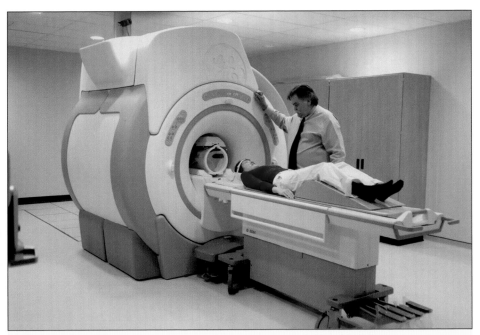

One of the most powerful MRI machines available today *(above)* is located at The Imaging Research Center at the University of Texas at Austin. An MRI machine provides an inside look at the human body to help doctors diagnose many diseases and medical conditions.

MRI scanner, doctors can see slight changes in soft tissue and even map the flow of blood in a patient's brain. A bonus is that unlike X-rays, MRIs have no potentially dangerous side effects for most patients.

Some Really Super Magnets

During the last few years, scientists and engineers have been working with a new type of magnet called a **superconducting** magnet. These work more or less in the same way as a regular electromagnet with one big difference. When a current flows through the coil of an electromagnet, there is a great deal of electrical resistance. It's because of this that a wire gets hot when a current flows through it. One of the problems with making very strong electromagnets is that the heat created by this resistance can cause them to overheat and may actually melt the coil.

Back in the early 1900s, scientists discovered that some conductors lose almost all of their electrical resistance when they get extremely cold. When this happens, they are called **superconductors** and electricity flows through them without creating any heat. The problem, however, is that most of these early superconductors had to be cooled down a lot—to below –450° Fahrenheit (–270° Celsius). This was not practical. Scientists continued to work on the problem and have been able to develop superconducting materials that work at higher temperatures. As a result, superconducting electromagnets are now being used in MRIs and other devices that need extremely strong magnetic fields.

Play It Again, Sam

Radar detectors, X-rays, CAT scans, MRIs, superconductors: these are all things that are very useful and have an effect on the way many people live. Yet electromagnetism also has a place in the daily life of an average person, a person who does not work as an air traffic controller or a doctor. In fact, one of the most important uses of electromagnets in modern times is for the storage of data, sounds, and images.

The invention of the phonograph was a marvel at the time, because suddenly a person could listen to his favorite song without needing to go to a concert to do so. Indeed, records were good for playing back sounds, but there was room in this invention for improvement: a person could not yet record sounds on a record. In 1899 a Danish inventor named Valdemar Poulsen had created a way to record sound on a magnetized piece of steel tape and wire. Simple wire recorders were used in the early 1900s but they never really caught on. In the late 1920s inventors experimented with the idea of using paper tape coated with magnetic material, but the real breakthrough came after plastic was invented.

Modern recording tape is really nothing more than a thin strip of plastic coated with a layer of iron oxide. Another name for

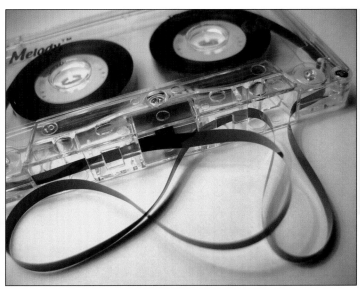

The cassette tape is just one example of a simple device that functions as a result of electromagnetism. Sound recordings are made on the magnetic tape.

iron oxide is just plain *rust*. When a sound is recorded on tape, a microphone first changes the sound—for example, a voice—into an electrical current. The current then goes to a device called the record head. The record head has a wire coil that creates a magnetic field when a current runs through it. The magnetic field in the record head magnetizes the iron oxide particles on the tape in a pattern that matches the sound. The same technology used to make sound recordings on audiotape is also used to record pictures on videotape and store data on floppy discs.

Once an audiotape has been recorded, the sound on it can be heard using a playback head. This device reads the pattern on the magnetized tape and turns it back into an electrical current. The current then travels to an **amplifier** and comes out as sound through a loudspeaker. Both radios and phonographs use an electric loudspeaker to produce sound. A speaker can be thought of as a microphone in reverse. When the electrical signal comes from an amplifier, it enters a coil of wire called the voice coil. The voice coil is set inside a circle-shaped, permanent magnet and is attached to a large paper or plastic cone. When electricity flows through the voice coil, it creates a magnetic field in the coil, which interacts with the magnetic field of the permanent magnet. This causes the cone to vibrate, producing a sound. As the intensity of the electrical current changes, different sounds are produced.

What's Next?

Given all the changes that have happened in technology during the last 50 years, it's dizzying to imagine what the future will bring when it comes to electromagnets. Here are just a few of the ways electromagnets will be changing the future.

MagLev: Travel on the Cutting Edge

Long before there were airplanes or cars, people would use trains to get around. Trains are great for moving people and cargo long distances, but they are noisy, the ride is not very smooth, and they are slow compared to airplanes. All of these problems are due to the fact that trains roll along on tracks. This is changing though, thanks to electromagnets and a new type of train called a MagLev. MagLev stands for *mag*netic *lev*itation. Instead of having wheels that roll along on rails like a normal a train, MagLevs float over the tracks and are held up by the force of electromagnets.

Recall the law of poles: if the same poles of two different magnets are brought near each other, they repel or push apart. This is exactly the principle that makes a MagLev work. Instead of having a track, these trains run over a "guideway." In the base of the guideway are strong electromagnets with their poles all turned in one direction. In the bottom of the train is a second set of electromagnets with their poles all turned the direction opposite to the magnets in the track. This means that where the two sets of magnets meet, the like poles will be facing each other. When electrical current is sent through the two sets of magnets, the train floats.

Since MagLev trains don't have wheels to roll on, they don't have regular engines to drive them. Instead, these use what is called a *linear induction motor*. Coils along the side of the train create a magnetic field that constantly changes direction. This

Japan Airlines's magnetic levitation train takes passengers between terminals. MagLev trains use electromagnetic force to propel them over tracks. They provide a much quieter and smoother ride than steel-wheeled trains.

interacts with the magnetic field created by a second set of electromagnetic coils in the guideway. A computer controls the timing of the changes in the magnetic field. This results in the train getting pulled and pushed along the guideway.

Because they don't roll on rails, MagLevs have a much smoother and quieter ride than regular trains. Plus, since there is no friction between the rails and the train wheels, they can reach much higher speeds, often faster than 300 miles per hour (480 km per hour). MagLev test trains have been running in Germany and Japan for more than 20 years, and a MagLev shuttle started carrying passengers at the airport in Birmingham, England, in 1984.

If all goes as planned, a new generation of MagLevs using superconducting magnets will be introduced in the next few years. It is

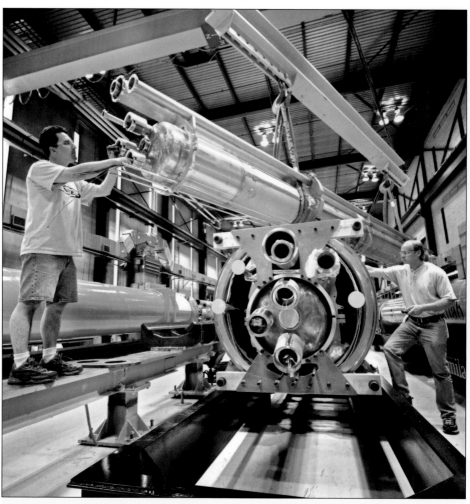

Technicians assemble a giant magnetic ring at the CERN atomic collider in Switzerland. This device uses superconducting magnets to accelerate tiny atomic particles at close to the speed of light. When the particles smash into a special target, scientists can learn more about what makes an atom.

estimated that these trains will have top speeds of faster than 500 miles per hour (800 km per hour) and use only a fraction of the energy that current MagLevs do.

Outer Space and Beyond

Using superconducting materials, NASA is drawing up plans to launch spacecraft using electromagnetic launchers. The idea behind this came from the recent discovery that when an electromagnet first gets powered up, it is not stable and pulses very quickly. The trick to using this to launch a spacecraft is to get the pulses of many electromagnets to all move in the same direction, allowing a shuttle to be flung into space.

Even though the use of magnetic rocket launchers may still be several years off, other devices using electromagnetic radiation are already being built. Cell phones and satellite television networks use microwaves to transmit their signals. New MRIs and CAT scanners are allowing doctors to get even better views inside the human body. Although the "death ray" dreamed up by the British Air Ministry may never become a reality, devices such as lasers and masers that use the same idea are already here.

The world has certainly come a long way from the days when the ancient Greek philosophers pondered the magic power of lodestones found lying on the ground. Scientists are only scratching the surface when it comes to understanding just what electromagnetism can do.

Glossary

alternating current (AC) – electrical current where the electrons change directions many times a second

amplifier – a device that makes a sound or electrical signal stronger

antenna – a device that receives or broadcasts different types of radio waves

atom – smallest part of an element that has all the properties of that element

battery – a device that uses a chemical reaction to make and store electricity

CAT scan – an advanced form of X-ray that produces 3-D images. CAT stands for computer axial tomography.

circuit – a continuous loop of conductors in which an electrical current flows

commutator – a device that reverses the flow of electrical current in a motor

conductor – a material that allows an electric current to freely flow through it

current electricity – a form of electricity in which electrons flow from one place to another

direct current (DC) – a kind of electrical current in which the electrons only flow in one direction. Batteries produce direct current.

electromagnet – a temporary magnet made from a coil of wire wrapped around an iron or steel core. When an electric current flows through the coil, the metal becomes a magnet.

electromagnetic field – the area surrounding an electromagnet where waves move out into space

electromagnetic induction – when a magnet moves past a coil of wire and creates an electric current

electromagnetic spectrum – a band of radiation having different wavelengths, ranging from radio waves at the low end to gamma rays at the high end

electromagnetic waves – energy that travels in space caused by rapidly moving electrons

electromagnetism – a basic force of nature involving the relationships between electricity and magnetism

electron – a negatively charged particle that usually orbits the nucleus of an atom

Faraday's Law – the number of loops in the coil controls the amount of voltage induced in a coil of wire and how often the magnetic field within the loops changes

frequency – a measure of the number of vibrations that a wave makes in one second

galvanometer – a device used for measuring a small amount of electric current

generator – a device that uses moving magnets and a coil of wire to produce an electric current

law of poles – the rule that states that the opposite sides of a magnet will attract and similar sides will repel

lines of force – the invisible area around a magnet in which the magnetic field is focused

magnetic domain – small areas inside a piece of metal that are lined up to turn the metal into a magnet

magnetic field – the area around a magnet in which the magnetic force can be measured

microwave – a type of radio wave that is used in radar systems and microwave ovens

magnetic resonance imager (MRI) – a device used by doctors to see details inside the human body

magnetron – a device found in radar systems and microwave ovens that produces extremely high frequency radio waves

nucleus – the central core of an atom that contains protons and neutrons

permanent magnet – a magnet in which the magnetic force is always present unless it is heated to extremely high temperatures

pole – one end of a magnet where the magnetic force is the strongest

radar – a device that uses radio waves to track moving objects some distance away. The word *radar* stands for "*ra*dio *d*etection *a*nd *r*anging."

radiation – energy that travels in the form of waves

radio wave – a form of electromagnetic radiation that has the longest wavelength and the shortest frequency

receiver – a device that picks up electromagnetic waves or electrical current. For example, a radio receiver converts radio waves to sound.

repel – to push apart

rotor – a magnet found inside an electric motor or generator that rotates or spins

spectrum – a band of electromagnetic radiation that goes from long waves to short waves. The visible light spectrum includes red, orange, yellow, green, blue, and violet light.

static electricity – a type of electricity in which electrons build up and stand along the surface of an object

stator – a magnet found inside an electric motor or generator that stays fixed in place

superconductor – a material that loses all its resistance to the flow of electrons when it is cooled to a low enough temperature

telegraph – a device used for transmitting messages over a long distance, usually using some type of code

temporary magnet – a magnet whose force can be turned on and off. An electromagnet is a temporary magnet.

transmitter – a device used to send electromagnetic waves or electronic signals out from a source. For example, a radio station uses a transmitter to send radio signals out.

vibrate – to move back and forth very quickly

visible light – a form of electromagnetic radiation that our eyes can detect

voltage – a measure of the amount of electric pressure caused when electrons build up or flow

wavelength – the distance between the top of one wave and the top of the next wave

X-ray – a form of high-energy electromagnetic radiation with a shorter wavelength than ultraviolet and a longer wavelength than gamma rays

Bibliography

Asimov, Isaac. *Understanding Physics*. New York: Dorset Press, 1966.

Editors of Consumer Guide. *The Big Book of How Things Work*. Lincolnwood, Ill.: Publications International, Ltd., 1994.

De Bono, Edward. *Eureka, An Illustrated History of Inventions From the Wheel to the Computer*. New York: Holt, Rinehart and Winston, 1974.

Essig, Mark. *Edison & The Electric Chair*. New York: Walker and Company, 2003.

Gribbin, John. *The Scientists*. New York: Random House, 2002.

Hewitt, Paul. *Conceptual Physics*. 8th ed. New York: Addison-Wesley, 1998.

Marcus, Abraham, and William Marcus. *Basic Electricity*. Englewood Cliffs, N.J.: Prentice Hall, 1974.

Macaulay, David. *The Way Things Work*. Boston: Houghton Mifflin Company, 1988.

Presence, Peter, ed. *Encyclopedia of Inventions*. Secaucus, N.J.: Chartwell Books Inc., 1976.

Tomecek, Steve. *Simple Attractions*. New York: Scientific American Books for Young Readers, W.H. Freeman and Co., 1995.

Tomecek, Steve. *Teaching Electricity Yes You Can!* New York: Scholastic Professional Books, 1999.

Tomecek, Stephen. *What a Great Idea! Inventions That Changed the World*. New York: Scholastic, 2003.

Williams, Trevor. *The Triumph of Invention*. London: Macdonald & Co, Ltd., 1987.

Wilson, Mitchell. *American Science and Invention*. New York: Bonanza Books, 1960.

Further Exploration

BOOKS

Delano, Marie. *Inventing the Future: A Photobiography of Thomas Alva Edison*. Washington D.C.: National Geographic Society, 2002.

Fullick, Ann. *Groundbreakers: Michael Faraday*. Chicago: Heinemann Library, Reed Educational and Professional Publishing, 2001.

Knapp, Brian. *Science Matter*. Vol. 5, *Springs and Magnets*. Danbury, Conn.: Grolier Educational Publishing, 2003.

Knapp, Brian. *Science Matter*. Vol. 25, *Changing Circuits*. Danbury, Conn.: Grolier Educational Publishing, 2003.

Levy, David, ed. *Scientific American's The Big Idea*. New York: ibooks Inc., 2001.

Parker, Steve, and Laura Buller. *Electricity*. New York: DK Publishing/Eyewitness Books, 2005.

Tomecek, Stephen. *What a Great Idea! Inventions That Changed the World*. New York: Scholastic, 2003.

Whalley, Margaret, and Kate Graham. *Electricity and Magnetism*. Minnetonka, Minn.: T&N Children's Publishing, 2004.

Williams, Brian. *Groundbreakers: Thomas Alva Edison*. Chicago: Heinemann Library, Reed Educational and Professional Publishing, 2001.

WEB SITES

Exploratorium: Science Snacks
http://www.exploratorium.edu/snacks/
Build scaled-down science projects based on exhibits found at the Exploratorium science museum.

The Mad Scientist Network
www.madsci.org
Submit questions about electromagnetism—or any other area of science—and get an answer from the scientists themselves.

How Electromagnetic Propulsion Will Work
http://science.howstuffworks.com/electromagnetic-propulsion.htm
Learn more about how electromagnets can be used to launch spacecraft.

How Electric Motors Work
http://electronics.howstuffworks.com/motor.htm
Explore a multimedia presentation of text, diagrams, and video explaining how different kinds of electric motors work.

Index

About the Author

STEPHEN M. TOMECEK is a scientist and the author of more than 30 nonfiction books for both children and teachers. He is the founder and executive director of Science Plus Inc., a company that provides staff development and enrichment programs to schools throughout the United States. He also works as a consultant and writer for National Geographic Society, Scholastic, and Discovery Communications. Tomecek was the writer and host of the Emmy Award-winning television series *Dr. Dad's Phantastic Physical Phenomena* and the science host for WNYC's *New York Kids* radio show in New York City.

Picture Credits